Live Your Faith at Work

Build a Bold, Christ–Centered Workplace Culture

What readers say about
Christian Business Almanac

An essential tool for anyone looking to lead with faith and purpose in the marketplace.
   Mark Whitacre, Vice President of Culture & Care, Executive Director of the t-factor Initiative, Coca-Cola Consolidated, Inc.

A masterpiece that supports and uplifts Christian business leaders in their daily endeavors.
 Krystal Parker, President, US Christian Chamber of Commerce

A tremendous compilation of scripture, practical advice, and Godly inspiration.
   William Bronchick, attorney & bestselling real estate and business author

A splendid addition to anyone's desk to capture life and faith in an extraordinary context.
   John B. Edwards, author, law enforcement expert

Daily bread for business owners.
   Michelle Ogden, wealth advisor, founder & CEO, Ogden Wealth LLC

The year-long journey every Christian entrepreneur and leader needs.
   Michele Miles, founder, She's Balanced

Jacquelyn Lynn has masterfully crafted a resource that not only nurtures my faith but also propels my business forward.
   Kim M. Clark, author; publisher, Deep Waters Books; podcaster; marketing strategist

The book that I didn't know I needed.
   John Crossman, author, Founder & President, CrossMarc Services and Crossman Career Builders

Our Gift to You

Practice Joy

44 Simple Daily Choices to Create a More Joyful Life

A practical, easy-to-use guide for cultivating joy through small, intentional choices you can start making today—without adding pressure, time commitments, or unrealistic expectations.

This free ebook gives you 44 simple, practical choices you can apply immediately to bring more joy into everyday life—clear, doable actions that help joy become a habit instead of a reaction.

Download your free copy

CreateTeachInspire.com/pj

Christian Almanac

Live Your Faith at Work

Build a Bold, Christ-Centered Workplace Culture

A Christian Business Almanac Focus Book

Jacquelyn Lynn

Live Your Faith at Work: Build a Bold, Christ-Centered Workplace Culture

© 2026 Jacquelyn Lynn

All rights reserved.

No portion of this book may be reproduced in any form without written permission from the publisher or author, except as permitted by U.S. copyright law. Send permission requests to info@contacttcs.com.

This book is part of the Christian Almanac series, a collection of practical, faith-centered resources designed to help Christians apply biblical principles in everyday life.

For bulk orders, contact info@createteachinspire.com.

ISBN:
978-1-941826-53-9 (paperback)
978-1-941826-54-6 (ebook)
978-1-941826-55-3 (audiobook)

Library of Congress Control Number: 2025928103

This book is provided for general informational and educational purposes only. It is not intended as legal, human resources, financial, tax, or other professional advice. The ideas and principles shared are meant to encourage thoughtful reflection; however, individual circumstances vary. Readers who need specific legal, human resources, or other professional guidance should consult a qualified professional who can address their particular situation.

Scripture quotations in this book are taken from the following translations:

Scripture quotations marked **NIV** are taken from the Holy Bible, *New International Version®*. Copyright © 1973, 1978, 1984, 2011 by Biblica, Inc.™ Used by permission. All rights reserved worldwide.

Scripture quotations marked **NKJV** are taken from the Holy Bible, *New King James Version®*. Copyright © 1982 by Thomas Nelson. Used by permission. All rights reserved.

Scripture quotations marked **NLT** are taken from the Holy Bible, *New Living Translation®*. Copyright © 1996, 2004, 2015 by Tyndale House Foundation. Used by permission of Tyndale House Publishers, Inc., Carol Stream, Illinois 60188. All rights reserved.

Scripture quotations marked **NRSVUE** are taken from the Holy Bible, *New Revised Standard Version, Updated Edition*. Copyright © 2021 National Council of Churches of Christ in the United States of America. Used by permission. All rights reserved.

Cover design: Jerry D. Clement

Interior design and production: Tuscawilla Creative Services, LLC

Published under the Create! Teach! Inspire! imprint

Tuscawilla Creative Services, LLC, Winter Springs, FL

CreateTeachInspire.com

"And you yourself must be an example to them by doing good works of every kind. Let everything you do reflect the integrity and seriousness of your teaching. Then those who oppose us will be ashamed and have nothing bad to say about us."

Titus 2:7–8 (NLT)

Contents

About the Focus Books	13
Why Faith in the Workplace Matters	15
Part 1 Create a Christian Culture	**19**
Purpose, mission, vision, values	22
Policies and practices	25
Operate with integrity always, even when it costs you	32
Build service and generosity into your culture	34
Treat people as image-bearers of God	36
Part 2 The Small Steps that Become Giant Leaps	**39**
Pray over your work	43
Make Scripture part of your décor	46
Integrate Scripture into other parts of your space and tools	49
Add a Bible verse or faith-based line to your email signature	51
Play Christian music	54
Create a prayer space and accept prayer requests	56
Offer a weekly prayer or devotional huddle	58
Pray with people in real time	60
Have Christian resources available to give away	62

Offer Bible studies and other opportunities for spiritual development	65
Establish a confidential emergency fund for employees	67
Provide access to a chaplain	69
Tell prospective employees about your faith-based culture	72
Offer volunteer time off (VTO) as an employee benefit	74
Provide opportunities to serve	76
Community service activities that work well for businesses	78
Create a climate of peace and trust rather than panic and fear	82
Honor the Sabbath, but work in the real world	84
Set policies that promote work-life integration	86
Provide professional development opportunities	89
Make space for God-honoring conversations	91
Operate with generosity, not scarcity	92
The Next Step is Yours	**93**
About the Christian Almanac Series	97

About the Focus Books

Christian Business Almanac is a page-a-day guide created to support steady growth—personally, professionally, and spiritually. Each day's reading is intentionally brief and focused, offering timeless insight that remains relevant year after year. Designed for busy leaders, it can be read in just a few minutes a day, making consistent engagement both practical and sustainable.

Today's leaders are navigating full calendars, constant demands, and competing priorities. Few have the margin for long, theoretical treatments, yet the need for wise, faith-centered guidance has never been greater. That reality shaped both Christian Business Almanac and the Focus books within the Christian Almanac series: compact resources that respect your time while delivering meaningful value.

Some of the daily topics introduced in *Christian Business Almanac* naturally invite

Live Your Faith at Work

deeper exploration. The Focus books exist for that purpose. Each volume takes a single essential idea and expands it just enough to provide clarity, direction, and next steps—without requiring a significant time commitment.

These brief books are written for Kingdom-driven leaders who want more than inspiration alone. You'll find principles rooted in Scripture, shaped by real-world experience, and translated into practical guidance you can apply quickly and confidently in your work and leadership.

Whether you read these volumes alongside *Christian Business Almanac* or on their own, my prayer is that they equip you to live out your faith with intention—in your decisions, your leadership, and the work God has entrusted to you.

Jacquelyn Lynn

Why Faith in the Workplace Matters

Christian business leaders genuinely want to reflect Christ well in the places he has entrusted to us. That desire creates one of the most common challenges we face: how do we create an environment that serves customers with excellence, treats suppliers and employees with integrity, and still honors God in everything we do?

At the same time, we can't ignore that the broader spiritual landscape is shifting. Church attendance in the United States has been declining for decades. The Pew Research Center's 2023 *Religious Landscape Study* reports that 62 percent of U.S. adults now identify as Christian, down from 78 percent in 2007. Gallup reports that weekly or near-weekly church attendance fell from 42 percent in the early 2000s (2000–2003) to

38 percent by 2011–2013—and to just 30 percent by 2021–2023.

A 2024 study from the University of Chicago's Becker Friedman Institute adds another layer of insight. Using anonymous smartphone location data, researchers found that about 73 percent of Americans enter a place of worship at least once a year on their primary worship day, but only about 5 percent attend weekly. That contrasts sharply with the roughly 22 percent who report weekly attendance when surveyed.

While faith affiliation and church attendance may be changing, our mission as Christians is not. Jesus said, *"Let your light shine before others, that they may see your good deeds and glorify your Father in heaven"* (Matthew 5:16, NIV). Whether people attend church every week or rarely step inside a sanctuary, they are still watching how believers live and work.

We don't need to get lost in statistical weeds to see the larger implication. Fewer people are gathering regularly in church, and that has significant consequences for how ministry happens. Most businesspeople—regardless of industry or job title—interact with more people in a single month than many pastors do in a full year of Sunday sermons.

That means your workplace matters.

Your influence matters.

And the way you live out your faith—whether you're serving customers at dawn, leading a team late at night, or navigating the everyday rhythms of your workday—may be one of the most powerful testimonies the people around you will ever see.

In the pages that follow, you'll find practical, thoughtful ways to live out your faith at work and project your character through your business so that your daily conduct becomes the kind of powerful, authentic testimony Jesus calls you to give.

Part 1 walks through how to establish a Christian culture at the organizational level, with principles that apply to businesses of every size—from solo operations to larger teams. Part 2 focuses on practical, day-to-day steps you can take to shape a workplace that reflects and honors God. Read with an open mind, and consider how God may be inviting you to begin right where you are.

Part 1

Create a Christian Culture

Operating with integrity is the foundation of creating a Christian culture in your business—but it's not the finish line. A faith-driven workplace grows when you intentionally invite God into every aspect of your operation and are willing to let the people you interact with know that you're doing it—and why. This isn't about religious performance or forced expressions of faith. It's about alignment. When your decisions, priorities, and practices are openly rooted in your faith, your culture becomes more than ethical; it becomes purposeful, consistent, and anchored in something greater than profit alone.

For a business to succeed, it must provide a product or service that solves a problem for its customers. Operating a faith-driven business also requires the understanding of how your business and your industry serves God's greater plan. When you know that, you can articulate your purpose, mission, and values.

Live Your Faith at Work

Purpose, mission, vision, values

Your company's identity and direction begin with your purpose, mission, vision, and values. Whether you're a solo entrepreneur or leading a multimillion-dollar organization, these statements should be crafted with care. When they're clear, complete, and shareable, they work together to give employees, customers, suppliers, and your broader marketplace a cohesive understanding of who you are and what you stand for.

Purpose explains why your company exists beyond making money. Profit matters—businesses that aren't profitable don't survive—but purpose points to something deeper. It reflects what God has called you and your business to do. It's the ultimate *why* behind your work.

Mission describes what your company does day by day to fulfill that God-given purpose. It clarifies the *what*, *who*, and *how* of your service to the marketplace.

Vision paints the picture of your long-term goals—what you hope the company will become and accomplish as you faithfully pursue your purpose.

Values define the core principles and ethics that guide your culture and behavior. Writing them down is essential but living them out is even more important. Values should be visible—modeled by leadership, reinforced throughout the organization, and recognized when they're demonstrated well.

Your purpose, mission, vision, and values statements must align—both with one another and with your faith.

Keep in mind that words carry weight, but only when they're lived out. Your purpose, mission, vision, and values must reflect who you truly are. If your actions contradict even one element, you weaken the credibility of everything else you claim.

Root them in scripture

Incorporating scripture into these statements reinforces your identity and helps you communicate a clear, consistent message. Choose verses or phrases that genuinely reflect your heart and your work. Since these statements should be concise, select scripture that captures the essence of your intention without overwhelming the message with a lengthy passage.

Create with intention

Developing these statements takes time—and it should. Be patient. Pray over them. Invite trusted people into the process. Share drafts and ask how the statements make them feel about doing business with you. Their reactions will help you refine the language until every line reflects your values and inspires others to be part of what God is doing through your company.

Once you've finalized these statements, share them widely. Communicate them to your employees, customers, and suppliers. Publish them on your website. Post them prominently around your facility. Let them be seen and understood—and let them hold you accountable to what you've declared.

Then the Lord answered me and said: Write the vision; make it plain on tablets, so that a runner may read it. (Habakkuk 2:2, NRSVUE)

And remember: these statements aren't "once and done." Periodically review your purpose, mission, vision, and values. As your business grows and evolves, revise them when appropriate so they continue to guide your work with clarity and conviction.

Policies and practices

With your purpose, mission, vision, and values clearly defined, the next step is to develop the policies and practices that will guide how you live them out every day.

Integrity and ethical conduct policy

Create a written, formal code of conduct that commits your organization to honesty, transparency, fair dealing, and accountability in everything you do. This document sets expectations, provides guidance when situations are unclear, and reinforces that integrity is not optional, it's foundational.

An effective code of conduct should be:
- Well organized, easy to read, and free from unnecessary technical or legal jargon
- Concise, while still comprehensive enough to address real situations
- Reviewed, acknowledged, and approved by senior leadership
- Accessible to employees, customers, suppliers, and investors

Your policy should clearly address behavioral expectations and practical areas such as sales and marketing practices, purchasing and vendor relationships, legal and regulatory compliance, respect in the workplace, anti-harassment and anti-discrimination standards, confidentiality, conflicts of interest, data protection, and appropriate use of company resources.

Equally important, include clear procedures for reporting concerns or violations. Employees need to know how to raise issues safely and confidentially, without fear of retaliation. Spell out consequences for violations and communicate a zero-tolerance stance toward fraud, deception, exploitation, or abuse of trust.

A written policy only matters if it is lived out. Leaders must model ethical behavior consistently and take action when standards are violated, regardless of position or performance. As Scripture reminds us, *"Whoever walks in integrity walks securely"* (Proverbs 10:9, NIV).

When integrity is clearly defined, openly communicated, and consistently enforced, it becomes more than a policy. It becomes part of your culture—and a visible reflection of your faith in action.

Establish people-first employment practices

People are image-bearers of God, not merely resources for productivity. Adopt employment policies that affirm the dignity and value of every employee. This includes fair and transparent compensation, timely and accurate pay, respectful workplace standards, reasonable work expectations, and clear paths for growth and development.

Put formal grievance and conflict-resolution processes in place so concerns can be raised safely and addressed consistently. Employees should know how to voice issues, who to go to, and what to expect from the process. When people believe they will be treated fairly—even in difficult situations—they are more likely to trust leadership and remain engaged.

A people-first approach also means fostering an environment where employees feel seen, heard, and empowered to do their best work. When policies reflect genuine care for people, they reinforce your stated values and demonstrate that your faith influences not just what you say, but how you operate every day.

Guidelines for faith-respect and expression

Create written guidelines that allow appropriate expressions of faith—such as voluntary prayer, faith-based conversations, workplace décor, or reasonable accommodation of religious observances—while also respecting diverse beliefs and maintaining a professional environment. These guidelines help set expectations, reduce misunderstandings, and protect everyone involved.

Emphasize that faith expression must always be voluntary and respectful. Participation in any faith-related activity should never be pressured, tracked, or tied to employment decisions. Likewise, employees should be free to decline participation without explanation or consequence.

Your guidelines should clearly address:

- Reasonable accommodation of sincerely held religious beliefs and practices
- Respectful, non-coercive faith-related conversations
- Prevention of harassment, intimidation, or exclusion based on belief or non-belief
- Equal treatment of all employees, regardless of religious views

Make it clear that professionalism applies to everyone. Expressions of faith should never disrupt work, create a hostile environment, or undermine mutual respect. Leaders play a key role here by modeling humility, discretion, and fairness in how faith is expressed and accommodated.

Scripture calls us to balance conviction with

respect: *"If it is possible, as far as it depends on you, live at peace with everyone"* (Romans 12:18, NIV).

When faith-respect guidelines are thoughtful and well communicated, they create space for genuine expression without division—allowing people to work together with dignity, clarity, and trust.

Set stewardship and responsibility standards

In addition to ethical conduct policies, establish clear standards that emphasize wise stewardship of financial, environmental, and relational resources. Stewardship recognizes that what you manage is entrusted to you by God and should be handled with care, foresight, and accountability.

These standards should address responsible budgeting, prudent use of resources, long-term planning, and compliance with applicable laws and regulations. They should also guide decision-making in ways that consider the impact on employees, customers, suppliers, communities, and future generations, not just short-term results.

Stewardship extends beyond money. It includes how you care for people, how you manage relationships, how you use natural resources, and how you safeguard the trust others place in your organization. Clear expectations help leaders and employees make consistent, values-aligned decisions when trade-offs are required.

Scripture frames stewardship as a responsibility, not an option: *"Now it is required that those who have been given a trust must prove faithful"* (1 Corinthians 4:2, NIV).

When stewardship and responsibility are defined and practiced consistently, they shape a culture that values sustainability, integrity, and long-term faithfulness over short-term gain.

Communicate in an honest, timely, clear manner

Nothing will destroy trust and confidence more quickly than dishonesty—even when it's motivated by good intentions. Establish clear expectations for how information is communicated with employees, customers, suppliers, and other stakeholders. Communication should be truthful, timely, and respectful.

Protecting confidential information is necessary, but it should never be used as an excuse for vague, misleading, or evasive communication. When people don't have accurate information, they fill in the gaps on their own—and those assumptions are often worse than reality.

Transparency, within appropriate boundaries, reduces fear and speculation.

Share good news openly so people can celebrate together. Just as important, share difficult news, upcoming changes, and explanations of how mistakes were made and addressed. If things are going well, say so. If there's a problem, communicate it clearly so others can understand the situation and, when appropriate, be part of the solution. Silence breeds uncertainty; clarity builds trust.

Scripture consistently links truthfulness with healthy relationships and strong leadership. *"Therefore each of you must put off falsehood and speak truthfully to your neighbor, for we are all members of one body"* (Ephesians 4:25, NIV). Paul is addressing how believers should live and work together, emphasizing that honesty strengthens unity and prevents harm within the community.

Clear, honest communication isn't just good management, it's a reflection of integrity. When people know they can trust what you say, confidence grows, collaboration improves, and your faith is reflected not only in what you believe, but in how you lead.

Live Your Faith at Work

Operate with integrity always, even when it costs you

Make operating with integrity the foundation of every aspect of your organization. Integrity is not situational. It doesn't change based on profit margins, pressure, or convenience. It's a commitment to do what is right—consistently, visibly, and even when no one can see you.

Always be honest, even when honesty is difficult or uncomfortable. Apply this standard to every area of your business: customer relationships, sales and marketing, negotiations, contracts, pricing, billing, and performance reviews. Resist the temptation to shade the truth, overpromise, or quietly omit information that might affect someone else's decision. In the short term, dishonesty may seem efficient; in the long term, it erodes trust, damages your reputation, and undermines your witness.

When you make a mistake, admit it and make it right. That may cost you time, money, or pride—but it also builds credibility. Customers and employees are far more likely to trust leaders who take responsibility rather than those who deflect blame or make excuses. Research in organizational behavior consistently shows that trust is strengthened when leaders acknowledge errors and act transparently to correct them.

Pay your employees fairly and on time. Fair compensation and timely pay are basic expressions of respect. The same principle applies to all financial obligations. Pay your vendors and suppliers on time, and if a situation arises where you cannot, contact the creditor before a bill is overdue and work toward a solution. Clear communication preserves relationships and demonstrates accountability.

Abide by both the letter and the spirit of the law. Not everything that is legal is ethical. Laws establish minimum standards; integrity calls you to higher ones. Refuse to exploit loopholes, manipulate technicalities, or operate in gray areas that conflict with your values. As a leader who represents Christ, your goal is not to see how close you can get to the line but how faithfully you can live above it.

"Better to have little, with godliness, than to be rich and dishonest" (Proverbs 16:8, NLT).

Integrity may not always be the most profitable option in the moment, but it pays dividends over time in trust, credibility, peace of mind, and long-term sustainability. More importantly, it honors God and reflects his character in a world that is often watching closely.

Build service and generosity into your culture

Just as you personally give of your time, talents, and treasures, use your company as a vehicle for generosity as well. Create clear, documented policies, procedures, and standards for your organization's philanthropic efforts. This may include charitable giving guidelines, matching gift programs, paid volunteer time, or company-sponsored service initiatives. Putting these elements in writing ensures that service and generosity are intentional, consistent, and not dependent on individual personalities or circumstances.

Many businesses choose to donate a defined percentage of profits to ministries, missions, or local charities as part of their ongoing financial planning. One important caveat: choose recipient organizations carefully. Avoid causes that are divisive or controversial, and don't allow generosity to become a source of internal conflict or distract from your core mission.

Consider offering deeply discounted or even free products or services to individuals or organizations that genuinely cannot afford them. This may include pro bono professional services, donated merchandise, other in-kind donations, or sponsored projects.

Encourage your team to participate in service projects and volunteer days. Invite employees to help select the causes you'll support. Shared service experiences strengthen teamwork, improve morale, and create meaningful connections between employees who might not normally work together.

You can also establish a matching gift program. Create clear guidelines for eligible organizations and a simple process for submitting requests. When employees see their personal generosity multiplied by their employer, it reinforces a culture of giving and shared purpose.

"Remember this: A farmer who plants only a few seeds will get a small crop. But the one who plants generously will get a generous crop" (2 Corinthians 9:6, NLT).

Make corporate generosity structured, sustainable, and sincere—not occasional or reactionary. While there are marketing and promotion benefits from corporate giving, your real goal should be to make this a natural extension of your values and a visible expression of your faith.

Treat people as image-bearers of God

See everyone—not only customers but also employees, suppliers, and even competitors—as who the Bible says they are: people made in the image of God, not simply the tools you need to run a successful company. Your "human resources" are human first, before they are resources. Let this perspective shape the tone of your leadership and govern all of your relationships, policies, and transactions.

"So God created human beings in his own image. In the image of God he created them; male and female he created them" (Genesis 1:27, NLT).

Recognizing the image of God in others changes how you speak, listen, and respond. It calls you to patience instead of irritation, respect instead of dismissal, and compassion instead of convenience. This doesn't mean avoiding hard conversations or lowering standards. It means addressing issues with dignity, fairness, and clarity—never with demeaning language, ridicule, or power plays.

Seeing people as image-bearers also affects how you handle conflict. Seek resolution rather than victory and choose reconciliation when possible. Reward patience, kindness, and service and do not tolerate gossip, cruelty, and disrespect.

When people are consistently treated as image-bearers of God, whether or not they are believers, it reflects how they respond to their work and to one another. When they feel seen, respected, and valued, they are more likely to take ownership of their responsibilities, extend respect to others, and act with integrity themselves. Treating people as who they were created to be brings a level of excellence that cannot be achieved any other way and lets your entire organization be a constant reflection of God in every aspect of the operation.

Part 2

The Small Steps that Become Giant Leaps

With your culture clearly defined and your high-level policies in place, you can turn your attention to the specific, day-to-day actions that bring those commitments to life. This is where intention becomes practice.

Small, consistent steps taken with purpose shape how your business serves employees, customers, suppliers, and the broader community. Individually, these actions may seem modest. Over time, they accumulate into something far more significant: a workplace that functions as a ministry not by title, but by how it treats people and conducts its work.

You don't need to do everything at once. Start where you are, act thoughtfully, and build momentum over time.

Don't assume that everyone in your organization needs or even wants the same things in a faith-based environment. Some will embrace your efforts enthusiastically. Others may respond with indifference. Even the same person may welcome one initiative and shrug at another. Accept that and let God guide you as you move through this process.

Faithfulness in the ordinary is often what produces the most meaningful and lasting impact.

Pray over your work

Make prayer your first action, not your last resort. Begin each day by praying for your team, your customers, and your suppliers. Lift up the people you work with by name and bring both their business needs and personal concerns before the Lord. Don't limit your prayers to what happens inside your office walls; include the family situations, health issues, and life transitions you know about. Thank God for what he has already done, and ask him to guide your decisions, attitudes, conversations, and actions.

A simple prayer journal can help you stay faithful and organized. It can be as basic as a handwritten list in a notebook or as structured as a digital file you update daily. Record names, needs, answers, and praises. Over time, this journal becomes a testimony of God's faithfulness—something you can look back on when you need encouragement.

Opening meetings with prayer

Consider opening meetings with prayer. Depending on your operation, this may or may not be practical—but many businesses find thoughtful ways to incorporate prayer without making anyone uncomfortable.

Live Your Faith at Work

Here are a few examples:
- **Small teams:** A brief, voluntary prayer before a staff meeting, inviting anyone who wishes to join.
- **One-on-one meetings:** Quietly praying with an employee or colleague who has shared a need and is open to being prayed for.
- **Project kickoffs:** A short prayer simply asking for wisdom, clarity, and unity as you begin.
- **Customer or vendor conversations:** When you know the other party shares your faith or has expressed a need, offering a quick prayer before starting the discussion.
- **Written communication:** For situations where spoken prayer isn't practical, you might send a short message such as "I'm praying for wisdom as we work through this together."

In larger or more diverse teams, you may decide that spoken prayer in formal meetings isn't appropriate. In those settings, you can still take a moment privately to pray before the meeting begins. The point is not to make a display—it's to intentionally invite God into your work.

Pray before responding in crises

When things get hectic or when crises arise, pause and pray before you jump into firefighting mode. The prayer doesn't have to be lengthy or eloquent. A quiet, sincere "Lord, guide me" can shift your perspective, calm your spirit, and help you respond with clarity instead of panic.

Let people know you've prayed for them

Whenever it's appropriate, let people know you've been praying for them—whether the situation is business-related or personal. You don't need to make a big announcement or turn it into a performance. A simple, confidential sentence such as "I've been praying for your situation" or "I prayed for your work on this project" can communicate deep care.

People remember that kind of compassion. It builds trust. It shows that your faith is not a slogan—it's the way you walk through the world. And when you consistently pray for the people you work with, your workplace becomes a place where God's presence is welcomed and his peace is felt.

Live Your Faith at Work

Make Scripture part of your décor

Post Bible verses in tasteful, visible ways in your office, conference room, lobby, or other appropriate places in your facility. Treat Scripture as a planned element of your furnishings, not as something taped or pinned to the wall as an afterthought. Verses can be professionally printed and framed, incorporated into wall art, etched onto plaques, or included in other well-designed decorative pieces that align with your overall aesthetic.

Choose short, encouraging passages that communicate a complete thought and fit naturally in a business environment. Themes such as wisdom, integrity, diligence, peace, and humility translate well in professional settings and are less likely to be misunderstood or taken out of context. Save longer or more theologically complex passages for Bible studies, devotionals, or small-group discussions.

Build an inventory of Scripture décor and rotate the pieces on a regular basis—monthly works well for many organizations. Move verses from room to room, swap framed pieces, or store some items for a season and reintroduce them later. The goal is intentionality. Rotating

Scripture helps people actually see and read the messages, rather than allowing familiarity to dull their impact.

As you select verses, keep the Christian calendar in mind. Scriptures about the crucifixion and resurrection are especially fitting during the Easter season, followed by verses about the Holy Spirit and the church around Pentecost. Passages celebrating the birth of Jesus are appropriate in December. This rhythm reinforces that your faith is alive and practiced, not static.

The Scriptures below are examples of short verses that work well in business settings. Each one is brief, self-contained, and translates naturally into workplace values such as diligence, integrity, accountability, and purpose without requiring additional explanation.

> *"Commit to the Lord whatever you do, and he will establish your plans."*
> *Proverbs 16:3, NIV*

> *"Work willingly at whatever you do, as though you were working for the Lord rather than for people."*
> *Colossians 3:23, NLT*

> *"Better is a little with righteousness, than vast revenues without justice."*
>
> *Proverbs 16:8, NKJV*

> *"Whoever walks in integrity walks securely, but whoever takes crooked paths will be found out."*
>
> *Proverbs 10:9, NIV*

> *"Do everything with love."*
>
> *1 Corinthians 16:14, NLT*

You might ask employees to submit their favorite Scriptures to use in your décor.

Used thoughtfully, Scripture in your physical space becomes a quiet but consistent witness. It signals what matters in your organization and gently reminds everyone—employees, customers, and visitors alike—that your work is grounded in something deeper than profit alone.

Build a Bold, Christ-Centered Workplace Culture

Integrate Scripture into other parts of your space and tools

Look for natural, appropriate ways to share Scripture beyond framed verses on the wall. Small, intentional touches can reinforce your values without overwhelming the environment. Some practical ideas include:

- Write a Bible verse on a whiteboard in the break room. Change it regularly so it continues to be noticed and read.
- If you have public signs you can update—such as a menu board in a restaurant, an easel-style sign outside your store, or windows you decorate with seasonal messages—include a short Bible verse or a brief portion of one.
- Use Scripture-based wallpapers or screensavers on shared monitors, digital signage, or company tablets that are visible in common areas.
- If you provide team members with company-branded items such as notebooks, pens, mugs, wall calendars, hats, or tote bags, consider including a short Scripture or a faith-based affirmation that reflects your values.
- Share images with Bible verses on your

social media channels, especially those that connect naturally to your work, your community, or the season.

Additional places to incorporate Scripture include:

- Inside the covers of employee handbooks or welcome packets.
- On internal bulletin boards or staff communication boards.
- In email newsletters or internal announcements.
- On packaging, product inserts, thank-you cards, or order confirmation materials, when appropriate.
- In meeting rooms, printed on small tabletop cards or displayed discreetly on shelves.

As with any expression of faith in the workplace, keep Scripture visible but not intrusive. The goal is consistency and sincerity.

When Scripture is integrated thoughtfully into everyday spaces and tools, it becomes part of the rhythm of work—present, steady, and quietly influential.

Add a Bible verse or faith-based line to your email signature

An email signature is a simple, low-effort way to express what matters to you and, when appropriate, to your organization. You may choose a verse that is especially meaningful to you and include it only in your own email, or you may select a standard verse or faith-based line to be used consistently across the company in email signatures, on invoices, proposals, and even your website. When applied intentionally, this creates a quiet but steady signal of your values.

If you don't adopt a company-wide verse, encourage individuals to add their own. This allows people to express their faith personally while staying within the overall culture you're building. As with any outward expression of faith at work, clarity and consistency matter. Keep the message brief, respectful, and professional.

The message doesn't have to be Scripture. A short quote from a widely recognized Christian leader or historical figure can communicate faith, character, and purpose without requiring explanation. Whether you choose Scripture or a quote, the goal is not to preach, but to reflect who you are and how you approach your work.

Below are examples that work well in an email signature because they are short, complete thoughts and translate naturally into a professional context.

Scripture examples

> *"The Lord gives wisdom; from his mouth come knowledge and understanding."*
> *Proverbs 2:6 (NIV)*

> *"Trust in the Lord with all your heart; do not depend on your own understanding."*
> *Proverbs 3:5 (NLT)*

> *"And whatever you do or say, do it as a representative of the Lord Jesus."*
> *Colossians 3:17a (NLT)*

Faith-based quote examples

> *"Faith is taking the first step even when you don't see the whole staircase." — Martin Luther King, Jr.*

> *"Pray as though everything depended on God. Work as though everything depended on you." — Attributed to St. Augustine*

"Integrity is doing the right thing, even when no one is watching." — *C. S. Lewis*

Kept short and intentional, a faith-based line in your email signature becomes a consistent reminder to you and to others that your work is done with purpose, integrity, and trust in God.

Consider changing the faith-based line periodically, as familiarity can cause even meaningful words to be overlooked or unintentionally ignored.

Play Christian music

If it's appropriate for music to be played in your facility, choose instrumental Christian or worship playlists. Instrumental music sets a tone without introducing lyrics that could distract from focused work or create discomfort for customers or employees who prefer quiet. Many organizations limit music to common areas—lobbies, hallways, restrooms, and break rooms—while keeping individual workspaces silent so people can concentrate. But even in those common areas, keep the volume at a level suitable to the environment.

Be mindful of copyright and licensing requirements. Playing music in a place of business is generally considered a "public performance" under U.S. copyright law, which means a commercial license is required. Blanket licenses are available through performing rights organizations such as ASCAP, BMI, SESAC, and GMR, which collectively represent most commercially released music. For many businesses, a simpler and more cost-effective option is to use a business-specific streaming service that either manages licensing on your behalf or offers royalty-free music designed for commercial settings. Examples include Pandora CloudCover, Soundtrack Your Brand (Spotify's business service), and SiriusXM for Business.

Very small operations sometimes play local Christian radio stations, but this approach still carries potential licensing considerations depending on factors such as the size of the facility, whether the space is open to the public, and the number of speakers used. In addition, broadcast radio gives you no control over content. Spoken segments, news breaks, fundraising appeals, or even a competitor's advertising can interrupt the atmosphere you are trying to create.

Remember that music should enhance the environment, not become a point of tension or distraction. When handled well, it can quietly reinforce the values you're building into your culture without a single word being spoken.

Live Your Faith at Work

Create a prayer space and accept prayer requests

If you have room, set up a small area that can serve as a prayer corner. Keep it simple—a small table and a chair are usually sufficient. If space is limited, a prayer shelf can work just as well, perhaps in a corner of a break room or another quiet area. On the table or shelf, include a Bible, a devotional, and possibly a few pamphlets or booklets on prayer. Add a simple sign inviting people to pray and to leave prayer requests.

Provide small cards and a box for prayer requests. The box should be lockable and opaque so requests can be submitted confidentially. Check the box regularly and pray over the requests you receive. Make it clear that requests may be anonymous. If someone chooses to include their name and it's appropriate to respond, let them know they are being prayed for. That simple acknowledgment can be deeply encouraging.

You may pray over these requests yourself, or you may choose to form a small prayer team. If you do, select team members carefully. Discretion, maturity, and consistency are essential. Establish clear expectations about confidentiality and develop a prayer rhythm that fits your operation, whether that means praying together daily, weekly, or as requests come in.

Depending on your type of business and facility layout, you may also make the prayer space available to customers or other visitors. In some settings, this can be a quiet witness to your values and a meaningful point of connection.

The prayer space should be accessible but not placed "center stage." Arrange it so those who want to pray can do so without drawing attention to themselves. The purpose is not visibility, but availability—creating a place where people can pause, reflect, and bring their concerns before God.

As Scripture reminds us, *"Do not be anxious about anything, but in every situation, by prayer and petition, with thanksgiving, present your requests to God"* (Philippians 4:6, NIV).

Handled with care and humility, a prayer space communicates that prayer is welcome, respected, and woven into the life of your organization—not as a performance, but as a genuine act of faith.

Offer a weekly prayer or devotional huddle

Give your team the option of sharing a brief time in prayer together each week. Choose a consistent time—such as Mondays at 8:00 a.m.—and keep it short, typically ten minutes or less.

Begin and end on time to respect everyone's schedule. Read a short Scripture, share a brief thought, and pray for the week ahead, the team and the work, and any specific requests that have been shared. This is not a Bible study; it's simply a few minutes set aside for prayer and reflection.

Make it clear that participation is voluntary and that no one is evaluated or tracked based on attendance. The purpose is to create an open invitation, not an expectation. Consider rotating leadership among willing participants so the gathering feels peer-led rather than top-down.

Hold the huddle in a neutral, accessible space, and keep the tone calm and respectful. Avoid turning it into a teaching session or a platform for announcements. Consistency, brevity, and humility matter more than eloquence.

Scripture encourages this kind of shared prayer: *"For where two or three gather in my name, there am I with them"* (Matthew 18:20, NIV).

When done well, a weekly prayer huddle

can become a quiet anchor point in the rhythm of work—a moment to pause, align priorities, and acknowledge dependence on God before the demands of the week take over.

Pray with people in real time

When someone shares a struggle, it's easy to say, "I'll pray for you," with good intentions. Sometimes you follow through. Often, the moment passes and the prayer never happens.

Try this instead: When an employee, customer, or anyone you encounter during your day shares a need, gently ask, *"Would you mind if I prayed with you for a moment?"*

If they say yes, do it right then. Keep the prayer soft and quiet—it's a prayer, not a performance. Make it short, simple, and focused on their need. Don't worry about being eloquent; simply name the situation and offer your request to God in plain language.

There's no requirement for physical contact. Let the situation and your relationship guide that decision, and if there's any uncertainty about whether touch would be appropriate, don't do it. Afterward, make a note so you can continue praying for them privately and follow up if appropriate.

If they say no, respect their answer without hesitation. Don't press the issue or explain yourself. A respectful response preserves trust and communicates care, even without prayer.

Praying in the moment matters because it meets people where they are. It communicates presence, compassion, and dependence on God—not just good intentions.

"Carry each other's burdens, and in this way you will fulfill the law of Christ" (Galatians 6:2, NIV).

Handled with humility and sensitivity, real-time prayer can become one of the most meaningful expressions of faith in your workday—quiet, sincere, and deeply personal.

Live Your Faith at Work

Have Christian resources available to give away

Stock an easily accessible space—such as a drawer, cabinet, or shelf—with Christian resources you can offer when appropriate for the relationship and situation.

This isn't about pushing an agenda; it's about offering help that aligns with who you are and what you value.

Some examples include:

- **A relevant book** – such as a devotional, a Christian business book, or a resource that speaks to a person's specific need (grief, stress, leadership, family challenges).
- **A short article or podcast episode** – especially one that addresses faith in the workplace, integrity, resilience, or purpose.
- **A scripture verse or passage** – shared in a handwritten note, text message, or email when the timing is right.
- **An invitation** – to a Bible study, church event, or community service opportunity, but only when you know it would be welcome.
- **Your own content** – if you produce

faith-based materials such as videos, newsletters, or books, share them sparingly and thoughtfully when they genuinely fit someone's situation.
- **Your own book** – if you're an author, give away copies of your faith-based book.
- **A prayer or worship playlist** – especially when someone is looking for peace, encouragement, or focus.
- **A local resource** – such as a Christian counselor, chaplaincy program, or church ministry if someone asks for deeper support.

The key is discernment. Offer resources that encourage and uplift without making anyone feel pressured. When your faith is woven naturally into your conversations and interactions, people can sense that it comes from a place of love, not obligation or expectation.

Let members of your team know the resources are there and encourage them to share appropriate items when the situation genuinely calls for it, whether with one another, customers, suppliers, or others who happen to be in your facility. These items should never be pushed or passed out indiscriminately; they are meant to be offered, not imposed. This isn't about distribution quotas; it's about being genuinely responsive. The goal is availability, not promotion.

Keep the selection current and in good condition, and periodically restock as items are used. Offering a tangible resource at the right moment can extend care beyond a conversation and give someone something to reflect on later. As Scripture says, *"Always be prepared to give an answer to everyone who asks you to give the reason for the hope that you have. But do this with gentleness and respect"* (1 Peter 3:15, NIV).

Offer Bible studies and other opportunities for spiritual development

If you have a large enough staff and adequate space, consider offering opportunities for spiritual growth. Bible studies, faith-based discussion groups, and similar activities should be held outside of normal working hours—before work, after work, or during lunch breaks—and participation must always be optional.

Encourage employees to step into leadership roles. When possible, identify two people who are willing to co-lead a group. This shared responsibility provides continuity and support, and it helps leaders grow together. Equip them with the resources they need, but don't expect them to have all the answers. In many cases, the most productive discussions come from leaders who ask thoughtful questions and guide conversation rather than lecture.

Start small. Smaller groups tend to foster deeper relationships and provide a more manageable environment for developing leadership skills. As interest grows, additional groups can be formed.

Set a clear schedule and scope. Avoid open-ended studies; define what will be studied and how long the group will meet. Consistency matters. Choose a regular day and time and commit to it, while also making it clear that perfect attendance is not required. Participants should feel welcome whenever they are able to attend.

Make prayer a consistent and foundational part of every meeting. Pray for the group itself and for individual needs that are shared, always respecting confidentiality.

Group leaders must be willing to prepare and commit the necessary time and energy. They also need to lead with humility, transparency, and vulnerability. Effective leaders know how to encourage participation while gently preventing stronger personalities from dominating the discussion.

Keep expectations realistic. Most participants will likely already be believers, and that's fine. Workplace Bible studies tend to focus more on discipleship than evangelism. Helping people grow, mature, and apply their faith in daily life is a meaningful and important outcome in itself.

Establish a confidential emergency fund for employees

Set up an emergency assistance fund to help employees who are facing a genuine crisis. Many households operate with little financial margin, and a single unexpected expense—a medical bill, car repair, or temporary loss of income—can quickly become overwhelming. An emergency fund allows you to respond with compassion in moments that matter.

Establish clear parameters for eligibility and how assistance will be requested or offered. Decide how situations will be evaluated and who will be involved in those decisions. Will employees need to apply, or will there be circumstances where you can offer help after becoming aware of a need? Whatever approach you choose, put guidelines in place that protect privacy and preserve the dignity of those receiving assistance.

Before moving forward, consult your accountant and attorney to determine the most appropriate legal and operational structure. Clarify how much assistance an employee may receive, how funds will be disbursed, and how those payments will be treated for tax and payroll purposes. Decide how the program will be funded—solely by the company or with optional contributions from others—and whether it will operate independently or as part of an existing employee assistance program.

The structure of the fund will depend largely on the size and complexity of your organization. A very small company may choose to provide assistance directly from operating funds on a case-by-case basis. Larger organizations may establish a private foundation, a public charity, or work with a third-party partner that specializes in administering employee hardship funds.

You'll also need to decide how visible the program should be. Some employers keep emergency assistance completely confidential, with employees unexpectedly receiving help when it's needed. Others communicate that the fund exists as part of the organization's culture of care, even if individual cases remain private.

Scripture speaks directly to this kind of practical support: *"Dear children, let us not love with words or speech but with actions and in truth"* (1 John 3:18, NIV).

When handled with discretion and wisdom, an emergency fund becomes more than financial assistance. It communicates that people matter, that hardship is met with compassion, and that faith is expressed not just in words, but in tangible care.

Provide access to a chaplain

Workplace chaplains are trained ministers who serve in business and corporate settings, offering confidential emotional, spiritual, and personal support to employees. Chaplain care can be provided on-site or off-site, and in person or virtually, depending on the needs and structure of your organization.

Some employees may already belong to a church and have a pastor they trust, but those pastors are often limited in their availability and may not be familiar with the realities of workplace pressures, organizational dynamics, or business-related conflicts. Other team members may not be connected to a church at all and may have no trusted resource to turn to during personal crises, family challenges, or difficult work situations. A workplace chaplain helps fill that gap by being present, accessible, and familiar with the context in which employees are working.

For employees, chaplains commonly provide support in areas such as:
- Emotional and mental health encouragement
- Crisis intervention during personal or family emergencies
- Conflict resolution and relational support

- Personal guidance during seasons of stress or transition

For employers, chaplain programs are often valued for contributing to:

- Improved morale and engagement
- Reduced absenteeism and turnover
- A stronger sense of care and connection within the organization
- Additional support for HR and management, particularly in sensitive situations

In addition to ongoing support, workplace chaplains may also officiate weddings, funerals, or other ceremonies at an employee's request, further strengthening trust and continuity of care.

Chaplains can be provided through third-party organizations on a contract basis, or you may choose to hire a chaplain directly as a part-time or full-time member of your team. The right approach will depend on the size of your company, your budget, and how integrated you want the role to be.

At its core, chaplaincy reflects a biblical principle of care and presence: *"Carry each other's burdens, and in this way you will fulfill the law of Christ"* (Galatians 6:2, NIV).

Providing access to a chaplain communicates that your organization values people as whole individuals—not just for what they produce, but for who they are and what they carry with them into the workplace.

Tell prospective employees about your faith-based culture

Not everyone wants to work in an overtly faith-driven environment, and that's okay. Being clear about your culture helps prospective employees decide whether your organization is a good fit for them—and it helps you avoid misunderstandings later.

Even if your faith-based culture is described on your website or in other materials, don't rely on candidates to absorb it on their own. During the first interview, clearly explain how faith is lived out in your workplace. If you open or close meetings with prayer, say so. If Scripture or other faith-based messages are part of your décor, point that out. If Bible studies, prayer groups, or devotional gatherings meet on the premises, make that clear. Don't assume candidates will notice or correctly interpret what they see during a walk-through.

At the same time, be explicit that participation in faith-based activities is voluntary. Make it clear that involvement is not a condition of employment and is not considered in performance evaluations or advancement decisions. Transparency on this point is essential.

As part of your hiring process, have candidates acknowledge in writing that you have explained your faith-based culture. This creates clarity for everyone involved and documents that expectations were communicated upfront. While most people appreciate honesty, it is a reality that some individuals later object to aspects of a workplace culture they previously accepted. Clear, written acknowledgment helps protect your organization and reinforces that nothing was hidden or misrepresented.

Being open about your faith-based culture is not about exclusion; it's about integrity. When expectations are clear from the beginning, you create a healthier workplace for everyone—those who stay and those who self-select out.

Offer volunteer time off (VTO) as an employee benefit

A popular employee benefit is paid time for employees to volunteer with charitable organizations or participate in other forms of community service. Volunteer time off (VTO) allows you to demonstrate your values in a tangible way that extends your impact beyond the walls of your business.

VTO functions much like vacation or sick leave. Employees are paid for approved hours spent volunteering, but clear guidelines are essential. As with any paid time off, you'll need policies that define how the benefit works and how it fits into normal operations.

Begin by identifying the goals of your VTO program. Are you primarily focused on increasing employee engagement and retention, attracting talent, strengthening community relationships, supporting causes aligned with your values, or some combination of these? Keeping your objectives in mind will help you shape the structure and scope of the program.

Determine how much time can be allotted each year. Consider both your budget and your operational capacity—what you can reasonably offer without disrupting the work that needs to be done. Many organizations start modestly, perhaps with four to eight hours per year, and expand the benefit over time based on participation and results.

Establish clear eligibility and usage guidelines. Decide who qualifies for VTO—full-time employees only, full- and part-time employees, or those who have reached a certain tenure. Clarify which types of volunteer activities and organizations are eligible and outline the approval process so expectations are clear on both sides.

Document the VTO policy carefully and communicate it consistently through employee handbooks, internal newsletters, and other company communications. Clarity encourages participation and prevents misunderstandings.

Finally, track the results. Look beyond the number of hours used and pay attention to outcomes—community impact, employee satisfaction, engagement, and feedback. Patterns and trends can help you refine the program and ensure it continues to serve both your people and your purpose.

VTO is a practical way to encourage service, generosity, and engagement with the broader community on company time, with company support.

Provide opportunities to serve

As Christians, serving others is part of who we are. The same should be true of faith-driven businesses. Service is not an add-on; it's a natural expression of values lived out in the marketplace.

From a practical standpoint, community service also benefits businesses in measurable ways. Well-structured service initiatives can contribute to:

- Enhanced brand reputation and customer loyalty
- Talent attraction and retention
- Employee development through teamwork, leadership, and skill-building
- Stronger networking opportunities and community partnerships

Beyond those benefits, service is a visible way to live out faith at work. It allows your organization to demonstrate God's love in action and to be salt and light in the communities you serve. Because of this, it's wise to put a clear structure around your company's service efforts.

Start by defining your goals. What do you want to accomplish through community service? Consider both the practical benefits to your organization and the real needs of the people or communities you hope to serve.

Invite employee input. Ask which causes

are important to them and what skills they can contribute or would like to develop. Involving your team increases engagement and helps ensure the service opportunities are meaningful rather than performative.

Identify potential recipient organizations carefully. Look for reputable local nonprofits that align with your values and objectives. Avoid organizations that are controversial or politically charged. If you or your employees choose to support those causes, it's best done individually rather than under the company's name.

Establish guidelines and policies for participation, time-off usage, and safety. Company-sponsored service should take place on company time or through a formal VTO program if you offer one. Make it clear that participation is always voluntary and that choosing to participate—or not—will have no impact on employment, evaluations, or advancement. Setting expectations up front protects both employees and the organization.

Finally, track participation and celebrate the impact. Share stories, acknowledge involvement, and highlight results. Doing so reinforces the importance of service and reminds everyone why it matters. As Scripture says, *"Let us not become weary in doing good, for at the proper time we will reap a harvest if we do not give up"*(Galatians 6:9, NIV).

Community service activities that work well for businesses

Hands-on service projects

- Serving meals or organizing food distribution at a local food bank
- Packing backpacks or school supplies for students
- Building or repairing homes with organizations like Habitat for Humanity
- Yard cleanup or minor home repairs for seniors, widows, or people with disabilities
- Community cleanups (parks, beaches, neighborhoods)
- Assembling hygiene kits, care packages, or disaster relief kits

Skills-based service (high impact, low cost)

- Providing pro bono professional services (accounting, legal, marketing, IT, HR, coaching)
- Resume reviews and mock interviews for job seekers

- Financial literacy or budgeting workshops
- Technology training for nonprofits or small community groups
- Mentoring students, young professionals, or entrepreneurs

Support for vulnerable populations

- Visiting nursing homes or assisted living facilities
- Writing encouragement cards for hospital patients, first responders, or deployed military members
- Hosting donation drives for clothing, coats, diapers, or school supplies
- Supporting shelters with meals, donations, or facility projects

Youth and education-focused service

- Reading programs or tutoring at local schools
- Career day participation or classroom guest speaking
- Sponsoring scholarships or school programs
- Coaching youth sports or after-school programs

Faith-aligned outreach

- Partnering with local churches or ministries for community events
- Supporting crisis pregnancy centers or family resource centers
- Assisting with holiday outreach programs (Thanksgiving meals, Christmas gifts)
- Supporting addiction recovery or reentry programs

Team-building service activities

- Group volunteer days with a single nonprofit
- Company-wide service challenges or service weeks
- "Adopt-a-cause" initiatives for a quarter or year
- Employee-led service projects aligned with approved causes

Low-barrier, flexible options

- Virtual volunteering (online tutoring, helplines, admin support)
- Donation matching for employee-selected charities

- Fundraising events tied to service outcomes

When selecting activities, the strongest results usually come from projects that:
- Align with your company's values and skills
- Allow employees to serve together
- Meet a real, defined community need
- Are optional and respectful of personal boundaries

These kinds of service opportunities make it easier for faith-driven businesses to live out generosity in ways that are practical, visible, and sustainable.

Create a climate of peace and trust rather than panic and fear

Lead from a place of trust that God will provide. Not everything will go smoothly. Markets shift. The economy cycles. Customers come and go. Suppliers make mistakes. Service failures happen. These are the realities of business, not signs that something has gone wrong spiritually or operationally.

How you respond to all circumstances, and especially to crises, sets the tone for your entire organization. Don't feed the understandable anxiety your team may feel. Instead, pray, plan, and then act. Address problems honestly, but avoid speculation, blame, or alarmist language. Focus on solutions rather than fear.

Your team will take cues from you, especially in moments of uncertainty. A calm, faith-grounded leader helps others feel secure even when outcomes aren't guaranteed.

Creating a culture of peace doesn't mean ignoring risk or avoiding hard conversations. It means leading with confidence, clarity, and trust, anchored in God rather than driven by fear.

When leaders model trust instead of fear, they create an environment where people can think clearly, work faithfully, and face change and challenges with resilience rather than dread.

When you stay grounded and composed, you signal safety. You're telling your team that challenges can be faced without panic and that faith informs decision-making even under pressure. Scripture reminds us, *"For God has not given us a spirit of fear, but of power, love, and a sound mind"* (2 Timothy 1:7, NKJV).

Honor the Sabbath, but work in the real world

Should your business be closed on Sundays? That decision requires balancing biblical principles of rest and worship with the practical realities of life and work.

Jesus made it clear that the Sabbath is intended to serve people, not burden them: *"The Sabbath was made for man, not man for the Sabbath"* (Mark 2:27, NIV). Rest is a gift from God, not a rigid rule designed to ignore human needs or responsibilities.

Closing on the Sabbath can be a visible witness to the world. It demonstrates a commitment to prioritizing faith and trusting God with provision. It also gives you and your team protected time for worship, fellowship, rest, and family—things that are often crowded out by the pace of work.

At the same time, there are legitimate reasons some businesses remain open, either fully or in a limited capacity. Essential services such as police, fire, and emergency medical care must continue. Other businesses meet real needs for people on the Sabbath, including healthcare, hospitality, transportation, and food services.

It's also important to recognize that not

everyone understands or observes the Sabbath in the same way. While most contemporary Christians consider Sunday to be the Sabbath, biblically, the Sabbath runs from sundown Friday to sundown Saturday. Some Christian denominations, including Seventh-day Adventists, observe Saturday as the Sabbath, based on God resting on the seventh day of creation. Respect the convictions of your employees when it comes to Sabbath observance, whatever day that may be for them.

Honoring the Sabbath is ultimately about creating space for rest, worship, and renewal. People of any faith—or even no faith—benefit from regular time away from work. That pause matters, even if it doesn't fall on Sunday.

Whether you choose to close, limit operations, or remain open, let your decision be guided by prayer and a sincere desire to honor God while serving people well in the real world.

Set policies that promote work-life integration

Work-life balance doesn't mean a perfect 50–50 split between professional and personal life. That's rarely realistic. The goal is a sustainable, satisfying proportion of work commitments and personal time. When that balance is healthier, both the company and its employees benefit.

The days of "leave your personal life at home" as a management philosophy are long gone—just as we don't leave our faith at the door when we arrive at work. People bring their whole selves to their jobs. Wise leaders acknowledge that reality and create structures that support it.

There are many practical ways to promote work-life harmony:

Offer flexible hours when possible. The goal is to get the work done well. If employees can shift their start and end times, work remotely, or use hybrid schedules while still meeting performance expectations, give them that flexibility. This won't work for every operation. Retail, manufacturing, healthcare, and hospitality businesses often require fixed staffing hours. But where flextime is feasible, it can be highly effective.

Focus on productivity and results rather than time spent at a desk. This must be coordinated with HR to ensure compensation remains fair and compliant with labor laws. When employees are trusted to manage their time and responsibilities, engagement and creativity often increase.

Review workloads regularly. Have ongoing conversations about responsibilities, deadlines, and obstacles. What worked six months ago may no longer be realistic. Adjustments are a sign of good leadership, not weakness.

Support employees' family responsibilities. Provide leave—hours, days, or weeks—that allows employees to attend important events, care for children or aging parents, welcome a new baby, or address personal matters that can't be handled outside normal work hours. Offer childcare assistance to whatever degree your organization can reasonably manage.

As you set policies that support families, be intentional about equity. Families come in many forms. Some employees have children. Others are caregivers for relatives. Some have fewer family obligations. Your benefits and policies should recognize these differences so that flexibility and support are offered fairly, not narrowly.

Provide the tools employees need to do their jobs. Don't require them to use personal phones, computers, or devices for work. Supplying appropriate equipment helps people disconnect when they're off the clock, protects company data, and reinforces healthy boundaries.

Make time off mandatory. Insist that employees take breaks, lunches, and days off. Rest is not optional for long-term wellbeing. Leaders should model this behavior themselves. While there will be seasons that require extra effort or longer hours, those periods should be temporary. If overwork becomes the norm, it's time to intervene.

This is not an exhaustive list. How you apply these principles will depend on your industry, size, and operational needs. The goal is not rigid balance, but thoughtful integration.

Stop viewing work and personal life as opposing forces. Instead, build a results-oriented, people-centered environment where productivity and wellbeing are allowed to happily coexist.

Provide professional development opportunities

Look for intentional ways to invest in your team so they can grow their expertise and apply new knowledge and skills to their work. This kind of investment strengthens the organization while also building loyalty, engagement, and retention among employees.

Effective professional development should address both hard and soft skills. Technical skills help people perform their specific roles well, while interpersonal skills—such as communication, collaboration, leadership, and problem-solving—shape how work gets done across the organization.

Practical ways to support professional growth include:

- Encourage employees to attend conferences, workshops, and industry events that deepen expertise and expand professional networks.
- Provide subscriptions to relevant publications, learning platforms, or professional services that support ongoing skill development.
- Host periodic lunch-and-learn sessions. Bring in outside experts when appropriate, and create space for employees to

teach and learn from one another.
- Consider offering tuition reimbursement or educational assistance as part of your benefits package, within defined guidelines.
- Implement internal development programs such as mentoring, coaching, job shadowing, and role rotations to broaden experience and prepare employees for future responsibilities.
- Acknowledge and reward participation. Recognize employees who take initiative in developing their skills and applying what they've learned to improve their work.

"Do you see someone skilled in their work? They will serve before kings; they will not serve before officials of low rank" (Proverbs 22:29, NIV).

Strategic workforce development is not a perk; it's a long-term investment. When employees see that their growth matters, recruitment improves, retention increases, and morale and productivity rise along with it.

Make space for God-honoring conversations

You don't have to preach at people. In fact, it's far better to let sermons come from the pulpit in church. But you can be openly faithful in ways that are natural, gracious, and sincere. When the moment fits, talk about what you've been praying for. Share a scripture that speaks directly to the situation at hand. Tell a brief story about how God worked in your life—how he protected you from making a serious mistake, opened a door you didn't expect, or gave clarity when you were wrestling with a difficult decision.

If someone is facing a challenge—whether it's a temporary frustration or a life-altering crisis—offer to pray with them. If they're open to it, pray right then. You don't need to make a big show of it; simply step aside where you won't be overheard and pray softly and sincerely. Let them know you'll continue praying and that you've added them to your prayer list. Then follow through. A quiet check-in a few days later *("I've been praying—how are things going?")* goes a long way toward building trust and showing genuine care.

Operate with generosity, not scarcity

Operate from the understanding that God owns it all and is able to replenish what you give. Let that belief show up in practical ways—paying reasonable wages, negotiating fairly with suppliers, sharing knowledge and opportunities, and giving generously of your resources.

Resist the temptation to hoard or operate from fear. A scarcity mindset leads to short-term thinking and erodes trust. Generosity, on the other hand, builds goodwill and reflects confidence in God's provision.

Don't clutch what you have to your chest. Hold it loosely, with open hands, trusting in God's faithfulness. As Scripture reminds us, *"And God is able to bless you abundantly, so that in all things at all times, having all that you need, you will abound in every good work"* (2 Corinthians 9:8, NIV).

Operating with generosity doesn't mean being careless or unwise. It means choosing trust over fear and allowing faith to shape how you steward what has been entrusted to you.

The Next Step is Yours

What you've seen in these suggestions is not a checklist to complete or a formula to follow. It's a framework for living out your faith through the everyday operations of your business. Some of these ideas will be a natural fit for your organization right now; others may be better suited for a later season—or not at all.

The goal is not perfection. It's alignment. When your beliefs, your policies, and your daily decisions are moving in the same direction, your faith becomes visible without being forced. People notice consistency. They notice integrity. And they notice when care for people is more than talk.

Start small. Choose one or two steps you can implement thoughtfully and do them well. As those practices become part of your culture, additional opportunities will surface naturally. You can try more of the ideas presented here, or you might see strategies in action in other companies that you can try. Over time, small, faithful choices compound into lasting impact.

What's essential to remember is that living your faith at work doesn't require grand gestures. It requires attention, humility, and persistence. When you steward what you've been given with intention and trust God with the results, your business can quietly and powerfully become a place where faith is not just stated—but lived.

If you found *Live Your Faith at Work* helpful, please leave a review wherever you purchased it.

Reviews help other readers and listeners discover trusted, faith-centered resources.

About the Christian Almanac Series

This book is part of the **Christian Almanac** series—a collection of practical, faith-centered resources designed to help Christians live out their faith in everyday life.

Each book in the Christian Almanac series stands on its own and may be read in any order. Some volumes offer broad, year-long guidance, while others take a closer look at specific topics related to faith, work, leadership, and family life. Together, they reflect a shared purpose: providing clear, Scripture-rooted insight that can be applied in real-world situations.

Certain books in the series are designated as **Focus** titles. These volumes explore selected themes in greater depth, offering expanded teaching and practical application for readers who want to go further in a particular area.

Whether you are reading one book or many, the goal remains the same—to equip, encourage, and support you as you seek to live with faith, wisdom, and integrity in every part of life.

Learn more at ChristianAlmanac.com.

JACQUELYN LYNN is an inspirational author, business writer and ghostwriter, and independent publisher who helps leaders integrate faith, purpose, and practical wisdom into their daily work.

She is the author of more than forty-five books, including *Christian Business Almanac*, and works with business owners, executives, and organizations through writing, publishing, and advisory services focused on values-driven leadership and workplace culture.

With decades of experience across multiple industries, Jacquelyn brings a grounded, practical perspective to her work. Her writing is rooted in Christian principles and designed to be applied in real-world business settings.

She and her husband, Jerry D. Clement, are the managers of Tuscawilla Creative Services, LLC, a boutique publishing and consulting firm that God owns in Central Florida. As a team, they write and produce their own books and assist their clients through all aspects of creating and publishing books and other materials.

Learn more and connect with them at
CreateTeachInspire.com

Jacquelyn and Jerry would love to continue to support you with their Shareable Saturday messages. Receive a scripture and inspirational thought delivered to your inbox every Saturday morning. Use the QR code or sign up at **CreateTeachInspire.com/ss.**

Take Your Faith at Work Even Further

Christian Business Almanac equips Christian entrepreneurs and business leaders with practical wisdom, daily insights, and real-world guidance for integrating faith and business all year long. Designed to support Kingdom-minded leadership, it addresses the challenges you face in the workplace with clarity, encouragement, and purpose.

Each entry helps you think differently about leadership, decision-making, people, and profit—through a distinctly Christian lens. It's a trusted companion for leaders who want their businesses to reflect their faith, not just in words, but in action.

If you're committed to honoring God through your work every day, *Christian Business Almanac* belongs on your desk.

Available in hard cover, paperback, and ebook editions everywhere fine books are sold.

Visit ChristianAlmanac.com for more details and purchase links.

CHRISTIAN ALMANAC
PODCAST

Christian Almanac Podcast: Where Faith Meets Real Life is a weekly podcast for Christians who want their faith to shape more than Sunday mornings.

Hosted by Jacquelyn Lynn, each concise episode tackles the real issues leaders, professionals, and business owners face every day—workplace decisions, leadership pressure, integrity challenges, relationships, purpose, and stewardship. This isn't abstract theology or motivational hype. It's practical, Scripture-grounded guidance for living out your faith where it matters most.

Every episode helps you identify a specific issue you may be facing and walk away with clear, actionable steps you can apply immediately—in your work, your leadership, and your life. The goal is simple: to help you live your faith with clarity, confidence, and consistency in the middle of real responsibilities.

If you're serious about integrating Christian faith into everyday decisions and you want encouragement that's thoughtful, grounded, and realistic, ***Christian Almanac Podcast*** was created for you.

Available on YouTube at Youtube.com/@ChristianAlmanac and all major podcast platforms.

www.ingramcontent.com/pod-product-compliance
Lightning Source LLC
Chambersburg PA
CBHW070154080526
44586CB00015B/1985